Study Guide
to the Apocrypha

Lane Burgland

CONCORDIA PUBLISHING HOUSE • SAINT LOUIS

Copyright © 2012 Concordia Publishing House
3558 S. Jefferson Ave., St. Louis, MO 63118-3968
1-800-325-3040 ♦ www.cph.org

Written by Lane Burgland

Edited by Ashley Bayless and Ed Engelbrecht

This publication may be available in braille, in large print, or on cassette tape for the visually impaired. Please allow 8 to 12 weeks for delivery. Write to Lutheran Blind Mission, 7550 Watson Road, St. Louis, MO 63119-4409; call toll-free 1-888-215-2455; or visit the Web site: www.blindmission.org.

Manufactured in the United States of America

2 3 4 5 6 7 8 9 10   21 20 19 18 17 16 15 14 13 12

Contents

Note to the Leader

Scripture alone serves as the only source and norm for doctrine and practice in our church. The books studied in this volume fall short of that standard. The first question that you, as the session leader, may face is this: "Why should we study the Apocrypha?"

We come together for these sessions to learn from those who have gone before us, concerning both what to avoid and what to imitate. New Testament authors do exactly the same thing when they direct readers to the Old Testament.

St. Paul, for example, points out that the events of the wilderness wanderings following the exodus were written down for our instruction (1 Corinthians 10:1–13). By their example, we learn to avoid the trap of taking our salvation for granted and thus running the risk of falling.

The author of Hebrews gives us a variety of positive role models when he lists people who trusted God and lived by faith, even when faced with terrible situations (Hebrews 11).

Their names may sound strange to us and we may not know the geography or history of the period as well, but we share a bond with the people who wrote the Apocrypha—a bond of faith and hope in the God who promised a Messiah, a Savior, to rule over us in an everlasting kingdom.

This study is not a verse-by-verse look at the books of the Apocrypha, nor is it even a chapter-by-chapter study. Instead, it will help readers gain a broad overview of the Apocrypha that will prepare them for class discussion and personal reading of these fascinating books. Make sure participants understand how to skim a book by reading through its outline and its headings. Many questions will take readers to specific passages to consider the writer's message and how it compares to things taught in the canonical Scriptures of the Old and New Testaments.

Be sure to open each session with prayer. You may want to include a short devotional based on a passage of Scripture that deals with the theme of the lesson you are reading. Encourage participants to share their stories as they read these works.

May the Holy Spirit bless you and guide you in the study of *The Apocrypha: The Lutheran Edition with Notes.*

Therefore, since we are surrounded by so great a cloud of witnesses, let us also lay aside every weight, and sin which clings so closely, and let us run with endurance the race that is set before us. Hebrews 12:1

1

Introduction and Susanna

Throughout the ages, Christians have recognized Holy Scripture as God's Word, inspired and inerrant. They were willing to pay the high cost of copying the manuscripts, and read the canonical books in a majority of congregations over many centuries, and risk death.

The people of God in the Early Church recognized the value of the thirty-nine Old Testament and twenty-seven New Testament canonical books. The Early Church did not always accept as Holy Scripture the works included in *The Apocrypha: The Lutheran Edition with Notes*, but they did value them and preserved them. These books reflect the struggle of God's people in the two centuries leading up to the birth of our Savior, Jesus Christ. God's people faced persecution, enduring all kinds of suffering rather than giving up their faith. They also dealt with temptation in the form of the allure of wealth and security offered in exchange for their faith.

The works contained in this volume carry their message of encouragement and hope to the children of God scattered throughout the world. They counsel us to trust in the Lord and do the right thing, even though the situation seems hopeless (as we will see in the story of Susanna at the end of this unit). Ultimately, God will deliver us.

Overview

1. Discuss briefly what you know about the books of the Apocrypha. Most Protestant Bibles published in the last two centuries don't even include them. After reading the "Foreword" by Dr. Paul Maier in *The Apocrypha: The Lutheran Edition with Notes* (pp. xv–xviii), why might it be a good idea to study them?

2. The contents of the Apocrypha vary from book to book, but as you glance through the front matter article "Features of *The Apocrypha*" (pp. xxvi–xxvii), what do you see that looks familiar?

A "Lutheran" Apocrypha?

When we read the Apocrypha, we join a long line of Christians who have valued these works and found in them some benefit for their walk with the Lord. As Lutherans, we bring to this task a deep appreciation for several key doctrines. Standing on the foundational truth that we are saved by grace through faith alone, we read these texts through the lens of the proper distinction between Law and Gospel.

3. Read the "Editor's Preface" (pp. xxi–xxiii) and highlight the two or three most important benefits, in your opinion, that we gain from reading these books.

The Background

A great deal can happen in four hundred years. Take New York City, for example. Today it ranks as the most densely populated metropolis in the United States, with over twenty million inhabitants. Four hundred years ago, however, the largest population in the area was beaver. The American Indians in the area raised crops and fished in the many waterways. Consider all that happened in the intervening four centuries!

In the same way, a lot happened in Israel between the end of the Old Testament and the beginning of the New Testament eras. The last prophet, Malachi, appeared at the end of the fifth century BC. A little over four hundred years later, Mary gave birth to the Christ Child.

4. Read "Getting Started" (pp. xxxiii–xxxiv) and identify some of the changes that took place between Malachi and the birth of Jesus. What are the most important events?

The Journey Begins—Susanna

Have you ever been between a rock and a hard place? That is, have you ever found yourself in a no-win situation? Susanna found herself in just such a predicament in this book. Through no fault of her own, she faced two equally appalling options. Read the Book of Susanna (pp. 243–45) and answer the following questions:

5. What does it mean to fear the Lord (v. 2)?

6. What choice does Susanna have to make (vv. 22–23)?

7. How do the actions of the elders and the outcome of the story prove the point of James 1:14–15?

8. Susanna rejects the elders and calls for help, although she knows she will be condemned and executed. Why does she do what is right?

9. In response to her prayer, what does God do to help her (vv. 44–46)? Discuss whether the Lord always answers desperate prayers in this way.

10. Who is Daniel?

11. Like a good detective, Daniel separates the two elders before questioning them. What detail reveals the truth?

12. How does the punishment fit the crime for the two elders?

13. How would this story be helpful to people facing persecution for their faith?

14. In what way does this story help you in your daily walk with the Lord?

Skim Ecclesiasticus for next time, looking for major themes. (You may find the outline and subheadings helpful for this assignment.)

2

Ecclesiasticus
(Wisdom of Jesus Son of Sirach)

The Fear of the Lord

The psalmist writes, "The fear of the LORD is the beginning of wisdom" (Psalm 111:10; see Ecclesiasticus 1:14). The author of Ecclesiasticus uses the phrase "the fear of the LORD" over twenty times in his book, indicating how important it is to him. To the modern ear, this may sound like pure Law. As we read Scripture, however, we realize that "the fear of the LORD" includes much more.

15. Read 2 Corinthians 5:9–11. How does the fear of the Lord include accountability to God?

16. In Proverbs 2:5 and 9:10, the author equates the "fear of the LORD" with "the knowledge of God" and "the knowledge of the Holy One." What does the knowledge of God include?

17. After studying Ecclesiasticus, do you think the author has a good grasp of the fear of the Lord and what it means in the life of the believer?

18. What, then, does the fear of the Lord signify?

Wisdom

The author of Ecclesiasticus used the word *wisdom* over five dozen times in his book. In the Old Testament, this term tends to occur in clusters: concerning Solomon (1 Kings 3–5; 2 Chronicles 9), in the books of Job, Proverbs, and Ecclesiastes, as well as in several of the prophetic books and a few psalms. Proverbs 8 provides the best introduction to Jesus son of Sirach's figure of wisdom because the author of Proverbs presents wisdom as a person. Like Proverbs 8, Ecclesiasticus also depicts wisdom as a person for dramatic effect. Although the figures of wisdom in both Proverbs and Ecclesiasticus have much in common, Jesus son of Sirach takes it one step further.

19. What does the figure of wisdom in Ecclesiasticus share with wisdom in Proverbs 8?

20. How is "the fear of the LORD" the beginning of wisdom (see Ecclesiasticus 1:14; Psalm 111:10)?

21. *Wisdom* is an abstract noun, yet the author of Ecclesiasticus has something concrete in mind when he writes about it. What is he writing about (see especially 15:1; 19:20; 24:23)?

Women

The Bible reflects a very positive view of women, although modern readers may not think so. Many in our Western culture eliminate the distinction between the roles of men and women and reject the biblical model of marriage (Genesis 2; Ephesians 5:21–33). Everyone who reads the Bible faces the challenge of separating our culture and our personal opinions from the worldview of Scripture.

In the Hebrew Scriptures and under the Mosaic code, women (like men) are human beings, created in God's image and likeness (Genesis 1:27). The Law applies the same penalty for the murder of a woman as it does for that of a man (Genesis 9:6). Although a woman's position in Jewish society was more difficult and restricted than a man's, she was a person in her own right. Women such as Deborah, Jael, Ruth, and Esther demonstrate a woman's capacity for leadership and heroic action for the sake of her people. Prophetesses, such as Huldah, could be consulted for guidance and advice (2 Kings 22:14).

22. Wisdom literature in the Near East often warns men about a number of dangers, including greed and alcohol abuse. According to chapter 9, what danger does a woman pose?

23. What status does a woman have in Ecclesiasticus 25–26?

24. How does Ecclesiasticus compare to the New Testament in its view of women?

Salvation

The Old Testament teaches us that payment for sin (atonement) requires blood sacrifice (Leviticus 1; 4; 16). It also reveals that we cannot save ourselves by works of the Law (see Paul's summary of Scripture's teaching on this topic in Romans 3:10–20). How does Ecclesiasticus treat the subject of our salvation?

25. Compare Ecclesiasticus 15:14–17 with Romans 3:19–20 and 7:14–25. What big difference do you see between Jesus son of Sirach and Paul on the subject of keeping the Law?

26. Read Ecclesiasticus 33:11–13 and contrast the doctrine of election presented there with Paul's presentation of that teaching in Romans 8:28–39 and Ephesians 1:1–14.

27. Holy Scripture teaches that the soul or spirit of a believer goes to heaven at the time of death and that all people, living and dead, will be raised on the Last Day and judged by Christ Jesus. What comfort does the author of Ecclesiasticus offer us in the face of our own mortality (see 17:27–28; 38:16–23)?

28. All Scripture points to Christ; He is the center of all Scripture. Does Ecclesiasticus point you to your Savior? Did you find God's promise of a Savior at the heart of Ecclesiasticus?

A Hymn in Honor of Our Ancestors

The author concludes with a hymn of praise to the Lord for the men of wisdom who faithfully stood at significant points in the history of God's people (44:1–50:24). He challenges readers to follow their example of faith and righteous living, resulting in God's approval and blessing.

29. The term *covenant* appears several times, especially at the beginning of this hymn. What is a covenant?

30. Ecclesiasticus includes Aaron, Phinehas, Samuel, and Simon son of Onias. What office did they occupy, and why does the author of Ecclesiasticus consider it important?

31. The author ends his work with a prayer of praise and thanksgiving and a final piece of wise advice. How would you summarize his conclusion (ch. 51)?

Review the outline for the Wisdom of Solomon and read through the ESV headings in the book so that it becomes familiar to you for next time.

3
The Wisdom of Solomon

During the time between the Old and New Testaments, the people of God often found themselves at odds with their surrounding culture, much as Christians do today. They found their faith especially tested in two ways. First, society pressured them via persecution to abandon their faith and value system. By a variety of means (financial penalties, social exclusion, and legal punishments), the world pushed God's people to leave their heritage, ignore God's Word, and change what they believed (see Jesus' parable of the sower and the seed that fell on rocky ground, Matthew 13:20–21). Second, their culture often offered incentives to turn away from the one true God and His Word. The world pulled God's children away from the Lord with financial, social, and other rewards (the seed that fell among thorns, Matthew 13:22).

This "double whammy" happened in Israel at various times, but the Jews in the rest of the Mediterranean world experienced it on a regular basis. Like islands of faith in the sea of unbelief, they constantly faced the temptation to give up the faith and adopt the religion and practices of their neighbors. The author of the Wisdom of Solomon writes his book, assuming the persona of King Solomon (who died a thousand years earlier), to encourage his brothers and sisters to remain in the faith and stay faithful to God's Word and their heritage. (The Book of Hebrews does the same thing, written to strengthen Jewish Christians in their faith.) Two thousand years later, we listen to the voice of a man who calls us to hang in, hang on, and not give up.

Righteousness (1:1–6:11)

In the Bible, we find the word *righteousness* used in two ways. On the one hand, we have what we might call the righteousness of justification. This refers to a right standing with God by which we are judged innocent of all wrongdoing and given credit for doing everything God requires. This "judicial" righteousness comes only by faith in Jesus Christ as the one who died and rose for us (see Romans 3:21–31). On the other hand, we have a righteousness of sanctification. The use of *righteousness* in this sense denotes the practical, daily application of saving faith in all that we say, think, and do. We encounter this meaning throughout the Scriptures, and it is often the way wisdom literature uses the term. As Christians, we have this in mind when we discuss the Law as rule or guide.

32. Read 2:1–11. The unrighteous reject the resurrection and deny life after death. Since they hope not be held accountable for their deeds in this life, they intend to spend their time in revelry, and they feel free to commit violence and robbery against the weak and helpless. What does the biblical doctrine of the resurrection teach us?

33. The unrighteous particularly target the righteous (2:12–20). Why?

34. Chapter 5 presents a picture of the righteous person, rewarded by God with resurrection to eternal life. It looks like the author of the Wisdom of Solomon teaches his readers that we earn eternal life by living according to God's Law. According to Scripture, how do you inherit eternal life? (See a similar question asked of Jesus in Luke 10:25–42.)

Wisdom (6:12–11:1)

35. In chapters 7–8, the author dons the persona of Solomon, the wisest of all people in antiquity. Compare these chapters with 1 Kings 3:6–14. For all of his wisdom, how did Solomon end up (see 1 Kings 11)?

36. Read Deuteronomy 17:14–20. What three things are forbidden the king, and what thing is required? How does Solomon, the wisest of all people, measure up to these requirements?

37. In your own words, describe what wisdom is. Then read and discuss 1 Corinthians 1:20–25.

God's Justice (11:2–19:22)

38. Compare Wisdom 11:2–14 with Exodus 7:14–24.How does God demonstrate perfect justice in the first plague against the Egyptians in the exodus story?

39. Some of the plagues against Egypt involved a proliferation of animals and insects (frogs, gnats, flies, locusts). How does the author of the Wisdom of Solomon defend these as appropriate (11:15–12:2)?

40. In chapter 12, the author of the Wisdom of Solomon points out that God gives people time to repent before He executes judgment (compare Genesis 15:12–16, where God informs Abraham about the exodus around five hundred years before it happens). Where and when does God fully punish sin?

41. The original readers of the Wisdom of Solomon faced trials and temptations to abandon faith in the Lord and worship the gods of the people around them. In chapters 13–15, the author points to the Egyptians at the time of the exodus and asks, "How did worship of creatures and nature work out for them?" How would you answer his question?

42. The author of the Wisdom of Solomon believes that God's people suffer only a little compared to the greater suffering of unbelievers. He illustrates this in 16:2–4. Following the exodus, the Israelites complained because they were hungry (Exodus 16). The author of the Wisdom of Solomon thinks it was intended to give them a small taste of the Egyptians' suffering. What was the greater lesson God wanted Israel to learn by its hunger and God's consequent gift of manna and quail?

43. In 16:5–14, the author of the Wisdom of Solomon uses the bronze snake episode (Numbers 21:4–9) to contrast God's rescue of the Israelites from snakes with the destruction of the Egyptians by the animal plagues. He points out that the true God, not the bronze serpent, delivered the people. What eventually happened to the bronze serpent, and what use does Jesus make of it (John 3:14–15)?

44. Modern readers have the benefit of electricity and all the lights made possible by technology. However, imagine three days in utter darkness (the ninth plague). In chapter 17, the author of the Wisdom of Solomon portrays idolatry as a darkness that robs people of reason, joy, and peace. Just as with people who panic in the dark, everything terrified the Egyptians (see Exodus 10:21–29). In the Wisdom of Solomon, the author's description of the Egyptians' panic might not be so farfetched after all. Read Isaiah 8:19–9:7. What breaks the darkness of idolatry?

45. The tenth and final plague during the exodus involved the death of the firstborn (the Passover; Exodus 11–12). The author of the Wisdom of Solomon argues that this plague was an appropriate response to a people who had tried to kill all the male babies of the Israelites (18:5–25; see Exodus 1:16). The Israelites also faced death, but Aaron interceded for them and atoned for their sin (see Numbers 16, especially vv. 46–47). How has the Lord interceded for your sins?

46. The author of the Wisdom of Solomon offers the reader a final contrast between Egypt (folly) and Israel (wisdom): the crossing of the Red Sea (Exodus 14). God used the same means (the Red Sea) to rescue His people as He did to stop the Egyptians. How does this comfort and encourage God's people today?

Skim over both Judith and Tobit for next time, taking time to read Judith 16 and Tobit 13.

4
Judith and Tobit

Surrounded by Gentiles, the people of God often struggled to keep and practice their faith. Some faced opposition in exile (such as in Babylon), while others faced persecution at home (for example, during Seleucid rule in Israel).

At times like these, people need a hero. We need someone to admire. We need someone to show us that all is not lost. Whether a valiant woman in the tradition of Deborah and Esther (Judith), or a devout man who risks everything to show respect for the Jewish dead (Tobit), Jewish authors gave God's people role models that taught valuable lessons: trust God, follow His commands, don't give up or give in. Like their original audience, we can find encouragement in these heroic stories.

Judith

In 1938, with the Great Depression in full swing, DC Comics published the first Superman comic book. Written by two Jewish men several years earlier (Jerry Siegel and Joe Shuster), Superman fought the minions of evil to preserve the American way of life. Everybody knew the character was fictional, but the nation needed an uplifting story in difficult times.

Like the creators of Superman, the author of Judith created a fictional hero to encourage the Jewish people of his day. Judith ("Jewish girl") fights the foreign oppressors with the help of her sidekick, "the maid." The bad guys are intentionally fictional but represent the very real Gentiles who ruled Israel so often in the period between the Testaments. Her message: trust God, remain faithful to His Word, and do what you have to do to win.

47. Read Judith 1:1–6. Take a look at the study notes for these verses in *The Apocrypha: The Lutheran Edition with Notes*. Why would the author make so many intentional errors?

48. Who is Holofernes and what is his mission (ch. 2)?

49. How could people save their lives and their cities in the face of Holofernes's great might (ch. 3)?

50. What action plan does Joakim, the high priest, develop for Judah and Jerusalem's defense (ch. 4)?

51. In chapters 5–6, Achior gives advice to Holofernes, who then delivers him to the residents of Bethulia. What point does Achior make in his conversation with Holofernes (see especially 5:17–18)?

52. What plan does Holofernes adopt for taking Bethulia (ch. 7)? Does it work?

53. What event involving Simeon, her ancestor, does Judith mention in 9:2–4? Why is this a problem?

54. How does Judith convince Holofernes that she is not a spy (ch. 11)?

55. How does Judith save Bethulia (ch. 13)?

Tobit

In *Antigone*, the Greek playwright Sophocles tells the story of a family torn apart by tragedy. The desire of Antigone to bury the body of her late brother Polynices can be helpful to us as we read Tobit. Because Polynices had been an enemy of the state, the king decrees that Polynices's body must lie unburied in the field. Antigone secretly buries her brother, but the king finds out and issues an execution order for Antigone. She hangs herself after being walled up alive because of her kindness toward the dead. The story shows how people of the ancient world felt a very strong sense of responsibility toward the dead and valued proper burial.

56. In chapter 1, Tobit describes himself as righteous, compliant with the Law, and compassionate toward the poor. What happens to him because of these qualities?

57. In chapter 2, Tobit hits rock bottom. Summarize his woes and the cause of them.

58. When both Tobit and Sarah are at their lowest point, they do something that eventually results in their rescue and restoration (ch. 3). What do they do, and why would it be important to Tobit's readers?

59. Compare Tobit 4:15a with Matthew 7:12. Which is easier to do?

60. In the story of Tobit, how does God deliver Tobias and Sarah? How does He heal Tobit of blindness?

61. Raphael counsels Tobit and Tobias, "Do good, and evil will not overtake you" (12:7b). Does God reward good works, and if so, how?

62. Both Judith (16:1–17) and Tobit (13:1–18) include a prayer of praise and thanksgiving to God for delivering them. How do you give thanks to God for His deliverance?

Read the Letter of Jeremiah and Bel and the Dragon. Also familiarize yourself with the biblical account of Esther for next time.

5

Baruch, the Letter of Jeremiah, Old Greek Esther, and Bel and the Dragon

Baruch

Have you ever survived a terrible experience and then tried to figure out what went wrong? Sometimes it's a matter of being in the wrong place at the wrong time. At other times, however, we can look at the events and decisions that led up to the disaster and see points where we could have done something different and avoided the problem.

God's people found themselves in just such a situation after Jerusalem fell to the Babylonians in 587 BC. They had thought God was on their side and that they could never be defeated. After all, they had the temple of the Lord, and He would never let anything happen to His house, would He?

63. According to Baruch, who bears responsibility for the calamity that befell Jerusalem (1:15–2:10)?

64. In his prayer for deliverance (2:11–3:8), why does Baruch think God should answer the people's prayer for help?

65. According to Baruch, where can we find true wisdom (3:9–4:4)?

66. What does Baruch say to comfort his readers in their suffering (4:5–5:9)?

67. How does this book bless its readers (*Baruch* means "blessed")?

The Letter of Jeremiah

Israel struggled with idolatry and immorality for centuries, falling prey to the allure of the religions practiced by surrounding nations. God sent prophet after prophet, calling the people to repentance. They refused to listen. As a result, the Babylonians destroyed their city and their temple, taking captive thousands of Jerusalem's citizens. Did God's people learn that idols bring only disaster? The author of this letter drives his point home with a jackhammer.

68. Why are idols a lie?

69. We don't ordinarily face the temptation to worship figures carved from wood or stone, yet idols abound in our culture. What modern idols can you identify, and why are they still a lie?

Old Greek Esther

When we read the biblical Book of Esther, we enter a world of strange names, distant geography, and unfamiliar history. As we read through it, we might notice something even more unusual: the author of biblical Esther never mentions God. The author(s) of Old Greek Esther sought to remedy that "oversight" by mentioning God frequently. They also added material about Esther and Mordecai and changed some of the other details as well (such as making Haman a Macedonian).

Note to the reader: Old Greek Esther can be a complicated book to navigate. See the chart on page 227 and the outline on page 229 of *The Apocrypha: The Lutheran Edition with Notes* for help in accessing the book.

70. The biblical Book of Esther doesn't explicitly mention God at work. Consider how God usually works in the world. Do you think that it's easy for people to see Him? Why or why not?

71. Why would the author of Old Greek Esther change Haman from an Agagite (Esther 3:1) to a Bougean/Macedonian (12:6; 16:10)?

72. Why would the author include Mordecai's dream (Additions A [11:2–12:6] and F [10:4–11:1])?

73. What lesson would readers of Old Greek Esther learn that they might miss in biblical Esther?

Bel and the Dragon

This three-part story reminds readers that God's people worship only the living God who made heaven and earth. It challenged Jewish people living in the midst of pagan culture to avoid the temptation of syncretism, blending the worship of false gods with the true God (see Exodus 34:10–14).

Eating plays a prominent role in this three-part addition to biblical Daniel. Bel, an idol, cannot eat because it is an inanimate object. The dragon can eat, but what it eats kills it. The lions usually eat, but won't eat Daniel. After Daniel leaves, they return to eating.

74. As in Susanna, Daniel plays the role of a good detective in the first story (vv. 1–22). How does Daniel prove to the king that Bel does not eat the offerings left on the table every day?

75. Read the story of Elijah versus the prophets of Baal in 1 Kings 18:16–40. What does this story have in common with the story of Daniel and the priests of Bel, and how are the two stories different from each other?

76. How did Daniel kill the dragon?

77. Read the story of Daniel in the lions' den (Daniel 6). What do both stories teach about God's care for His people?

Skim 1 Maccabees and review the book's outline, looking for main characters for next time.

6

1 Maccabees

How much do you know about the history of Israel during the time between the Testaments (400 BC–AD 50)? Most of us don't know it very well because we didn't study it in school and not many movies or television shows have been made about the time period.

The history of this period lays the foundation for understanding the New Testament. For example, why did the Jewish people expect a warrior-messiah like David? Who are the Pharisees, and why are they so serious about God's Law? Why is the New Testament written in Greek? Use the historical material in the front part of *The Apocrypha: The Lutheran Edition with Notes* (especially pp. lv–lxxv) to identify the people you will encounter in 1 Maccabees. Remember that they were very much like us: people that wanted to worship the one true God but had to find a way to do it in a world set against them.

The Problem (Chapter 1)

78. What impact did Alexander the Great have on Israel?

79. Who was Antiochus IV Epiphanes? What did he want to do in Israel?

80. What two distinguishing features of Judaism did Antiochus make punishable by the death penalty?

81. What is the "desolating sacrilege" mentioned in 1 Maccabees 1:54, and where does it appear in Holy Scripture?

Mattathias Reacts (Chapter 2)

82. What is the story behind Phinehas and Zimri mentioned in 1 Maccabees 2:26? What is the author's point?

83. In the "Last Words of Mattathias" (2:49–70), what great biblical doctrine is missing?

84. Compare Mattathias's admonition to "pay back the Gentiles in full" (2:68) with Jesus' command to forgive our enemies (Matthew 5:11–12, 43–48). Which comes more naturally to us?

Judas Maccabeus (3:1–9:22)

85. What is Hanukkah, and what does it celebrate (4:59)?

86. The Book of 1 Maccabees idealizes the Maccabean family and paints a picture of Judas Maccabeus as faithful, courageous, and shrewd. In 5:55–62, what does the author of this book point to as the cause of the victory for Israel?

87. How does the author's comment in 1 Maccabees 5:53 reflect the promise of Mattathias given years earlier (2:51)?

88. Things end up poorly for Judas Maccabeus, deserted by all but eight hundred men. Why does he fight rather than take the advice of his commanders (9:1–18)?

Jonathan (9:23–12:53)

89. Jonathan, Judas's successor, attacks a wedding party and kills most of them (9:37–42). Why?

90. How does the war between Jonathan and Bacchides end?

91. Jonathan succeeds his late brother Judas as military and political leader of the Jewish people. How does he also become high priest?

92. If Judas Maccabeus excelled as a military commander, what was Jonathan's claim to fame?

93. We see few references to the Lord or to Holy Scripture (12:9, 15 are notable exceptions). What do the Maccabees seem to depend on instead?

Simon (Chapters 13–16)

94. What did Simon accomplish to make his homeland secure?

95. What honors did the people bestow upon Simon in return?

96. How did Simon die?

97. During His public ministry, Jesus kept His messianic identity a secret. He revealed Himself to His disciples and a few Samaritans. How does 1 Maccabees help explain His reluctance to reveal Himself openly?

Skim over 2 Maccabees and then read the Prayer of Azariah, the Song of the Three Holy Children, and the Prayer of Manasseh for next time.

7

2 Maccabees and the Prayers and Songs

2 Maccabees

Moses offers Israel two paths. If they walk the path of covenant faithfulness, obeying the laws God gave them, then God will bless them materially and make sure their enemies go down in defeat (Deuteronomy 28:1–14). If they rebel against Him, ignoring His laws and decrees, then God will curse them with hunger, disaster, and foreign domination (Deuteronomy 28:15–68). The author of 2 Maccabees tells the story of the Jewish people in the first half of the second century BC in the light of covenantal blessings and curses. He also shows his readers the supreme importance of the temple as an object of God's favor and protection.

The Books of 1 and 2 Maccabees bear the same name and report the history of God's people during the difficult time of Seleucid rule in Judah (second century BC). However, three differences stand out. First, 1 Maccabees is an original work, while 2 Maccabees is an epitome (summary) of someone else's work. Second, 2 Maccabees concentrates on a shorter historical period (about 185–160 BC) than does 1 Maccabees (about 175–134 BC). Third, the author of 2 Maccabees shows less interest in validating the Maccabees as a ruling family, giving much more attention to the temple and God's approval of those who follow Jewish laws.

98. What goal does the author of 2 Maccabees have in mind as he writes to the Jewish expatriates in Egypt (1:18)?

99. What caused the first crisis at the temple, and how was it resolved (ch. 3)?

100. According to the author, what was the second crisis at the temple, and why didn't God intervene (5:15–27)?

101. Why did God let His people suffer so terribly under Antiochus IV Epiphanes (6:12–17)?

102. What did Eleazar refuse to do that cost him his life (6:18–20)? How did the teachings of Jesus address these cultural tensions? (See Mark 7:19.)

103. Eleazar refused to pretend that he was complying with the wishes of the foreign rulers, as some suggested he should (6:21). People watch what we do as Christians. Discuss some examples from our everyday lives in which people look for hypocrisy in Christians.

104. What "secret weapon" did Judas Maccabeus use when facing a larger army led by Nicanor (8:21–23)?

105. After the martyrdoms, the second crisis at the temple comes to a resolution. What happens to Antiochus IV Epiphanes (ch. 9)?

106. How does the author of 2 Maccabees explain the death in battle of certain Jewish soldiers (12:38–45)?

107. What is the third crisis (ch. 14)? How is it neutralized (ch. 15)?

The Prayer of Azariah and the Song of the Three Holy Children

The story in Daniel of the three Jewish men facing the threat of death has inspired God's people for centuries. When we read it, we realize that whether we live or die doesn't really matter that much. The important question is, rather, are we faithful to the Lord? (See Daniel 3:16–18.)

108. God's people have blessed the name of the Lord since the days of Abraham (see Genesis 14:20; 24:27). Even today, Jewish mealtime prayers begin with "Blessed art Thou, O Lord our God, King of the universe." Azariah, also known by his Babylonian name of Abednego, opens his prayer in the fiery furnace with "Blessed are You, O Lord" (v. 3). What does it mean to bless the name of the Lord?

109. Azariah confesses the sin of his people and acknowledges the justice of God's response (the fall of Jerusalem, the destruction of the temple, and the Babylonian captivity). How does this reflect both God's righteousness (Law) and His mercy (Gospel)?

110. When we get caught speeding, we get a ticket and pay a fine. Is that how it works when God catches us in a sin? Can we just pay a fine? (See Psalm 51.)

111. In the midst of the fiery furnace, the three faithful children of God sing a song of praise to the Lord who delivers them (vv. 23–68). Also consider the trial and stoning of Stephen in Acts 7. What lesson can we learn about facing the world's opposition to our faith?

The Prayer of Manasseh

Sometimes our sins overwhelm us. We feel like we are the worst sinner in the whole world. If Manasseh felt like this, he might see himself outside of God's covenant people. The term *righteous* could be taken in the ordinary sense of faithful obedience to God's covenant. In that case, God is a "God of the righteous" (v. 8) because of the covenant relationship He established at Mount Sinai through Moses. Those who keep the covenant would be righteous in the sense that they committed no great crimes deserving of death. The author of the Prayer of Manasseh makes a number of statements that stand in sharp contrast to the Scriptures (v. 8).

112. In light of his deep remorse, perhaps Manasseh is comparing himself to Abraham, Isaac, and Jacob. Read 2 Kings 21:1–18 and list some of Manasseh's grievances against the Lord. How do those compare to the lives of the patriarchs? (Or look at Paul's self-evaluation in 1 Timothy 1:12–17.) Have you ever felt like this?

113. If God is the "God of the righteous" (v. 8), how can He also be "the God of those who repent" (v. 13)?

114. In our era of self-assertion and positive thinking, we often drop Confession and Absolution from our worship services. How do these practices continue to have a place in our relationship with God? (See Luke 18:9–14.)

Epilogue

As you wrap up this study guide to the Apocrypha, we pray you are now better equipped to read through the full Apocrypha independently. We have given you the tools to gain the benefits as well as avoid the pitfalls of these books. We encourage you to continue your study by using the reading guide on pages xxviii–xxix at the front of *The Apocrypha: The Lutheran Edition with Notes.* This reading chart will guide you through about two chapters of the Apocrypha as well as a Bible reading each day. If the readings are too long for you, break them down and pace yourself. You could read one chapter a day, if you'd prefer.

We pray that God will continue to bless and guide you as you read and study *The Apocrypha: The Lutheran Edition with Notes.*

Leader Guide

1

Introduction and Susanna

Objectives

By the power of the Holy Spirit working through God's Word, participants will

- ◆ become better acquainted with the books of the Apocrypha;
- ◆ see value in reading them; and
- ◆ begin their journey through the Apocrypha by reading the Book of Susanna.

Overview

1. Many theologians in the Early Church accepted the apocryphal books as authoritative. Others, however, noted the differences between them and Holy Scripture. Luther offers us the best way to evaluate the books of the Apocrypha. He separated them from the Scriptures but included them in his German translation between the Testaments, suggesting they were good and useful to read even though they were not on par with Holy Scripture.

2. The works in *The Apocrypha: The Lutheran Edition with Notes* have been arranged in chapter and verse format, with subheadings to separate content and study notes to help the reader understand the text. New to *The Apocrypha* is the running chronology at the top of the page, identifying the date of the works or of the events.

A "Lutheran" Apocrypha?

3. The "Editor's Preface" lists several benefits that we, as Lutherans, receive in reading these works. Along with seeing the common bond of messianic faith in the lives of the Jews of the intertestamental period, as we share and learn something of their struggle for the faith in difficult

times, we have the opportunity to discuss two important themes. First, we want to interpret Scripture in its literary and historical context. Reading the Apocrypha, we can investigate how well those authors read and applied Holy Scripture to their situations. Second, we can gain firsthand experience in why our spiritual ancestors separated these books from Scripture. In an era when television programs try to convince people that the Christian Church simply "banned" certain books, we will appreciate the truth: the Apocrypha did not convince readers that these texts were inspired of God, inerrant, and authoritative. As session leader, you may want to guide the participants in a discussion of how the Scriptures authenticated themselves in the Early Church. The Church did not create the Bible; it merely recognized the Word of God as the Word of God, different from all other works.

The Background

As session leader, you may want to read through some of the historical material in *The Apocrypha: The Lutheran Edition with Notes* before you get together with the participants. It might be best to stick to a broad outline rather than get bogged down in details. The following timeline might be helpful:

Persian rule: 530–330 BC

Greek rule: 330–167 BC

Maccabean rule: 167–63 BC

Roman rule: 63 BC–AD 637

You can divide the Greek rule over Judea into the Ptolemaic period (323–198 BC) and the Seleucid period (198–164 BC). Life under the Ptolemies was generally peaceful, but the Seleucids pushed Hellenization much more aggressively. This led to the Maccabean revolt and the beginning of home rule.

4. Two things happened during these "silent years" that greatly impacted the New Testament era. First, Alexander the Great conquered the Mediterranean world, making Koine Greek the universal language of the area. This made evangelism possible in the first century AD because an apostle or missionary could communicate anywhere in the Mediterranean with this simplified form of Greek. Second, faithful

Jewish scholars translated the Hebrew Scriptures into this common language (resulting in the Septuagint). The Word of God now became available to everyone, Jew or Greek, regardless of his or her own native language. God used these two developments to lay the foundation for the Gospel explosion recorded in Acts and beyond.

The Journey Begins—Susanna

Homer's hero Odysseus faced a terrible choice on his voyage. He had to pass through a narrow strait, but a fierce whirlpool (Charybdis) lay on one side and a horrible monster (Scylla) inhabited the other side. He had to choose risking his entire ship and crew in the whirlpool or having some of his crew eaten by the six-headed monster on the other. Which would you choose? (He chose the monster, sacrificing some of his crew rather than risking them all.)

Susanna faced a similar dilemma. She could either yield to the corrupt elders or face humiliation and execution by their false testimony. Which should she do?

5. In both Old and New Testaments, the expression "fear the Lord" denotes trust and obedience, a comprehensive phrase that sums up the heart and life of a child of God. The author of Proverbs 9:10 provides the key when he equates "the fear of the LORD" with "knowledge of the Holy One."

"Fear of the LORD" describes a warm, personal relationship with the living God that permeates all areas of life and action. It serves as the foundation for true wisdom and is characteristic of the Messiah (see Isaiah 11:3).

6. It is a decision between presumed death by her countrymen or punishment from God. Susanna knows that people will believe the elders because they are powerful, respected men in the community. Because there are two of them, their witness against her will be legal in a capital case (Deuteronomy 17:6; adultery was a death-penalty crime, Leviticus 20:10; Deuteronomy 22:22).

7. As we see time and again, desire gives birth to sinful action, which always results in death (James 1:14–15). We learn a similar lesson from David and Bathsheba (2 Samuel 11) as well as from the story of Naboth's vineyard (1 Kings 21).

8. Susanna deeply and truly trusted the Lord (v. 35). We might say she looked beyond the immediate problem to the Lord and His eventual judgment. Had she opted for the short-sighted solution (accede to the demands of the elders), she would have been guilty before the Lord of a crime deserving death. Her faith led her to make the hard decision, in a way similar to the three men in Daniel 3 (see especially vv. 16–18).

9. The Lord rouses Daniel and sends him like a "knight in shining armor" to rescue Susanna. However, sometimes God allows the miscarriage of justice (as in the case of Naboth, 1 Kings 21).

10. Daniel was a young Jewish man of high rank who was taken to Babylon in the first deportation (about 600 BC). His faithfulness to the Lord made him a legend among the people of God and a model for believers living under persecution.

11. The two elders had not had time to work out all the details of their story. Under separate questioning, they differed as to the type of tree under which Susanna allegedly committed adultery.

12. What they would have done to Susanna is now done to them (as prescribed in Deuteronomy 19:16–21). The author of Susanna also creates a word play between the type of tree described by each elder and the punishment God would render to them, emphasizing the appropriate nature of the punishment.

13. Like Susanna, Jewish people facing persecution had two choices. They could deny their faith and save their lives (equivalent to giving in to the two elders) or confess their faith and face the consequences (often severe; remember Peter's decision, Luke 22:54–62). The story of Susanna challenged them to look beyond their immediate personal welfare to the God who is able to save their souls eternally.

14. Like the original readers of Hebrews, we have not yet faced opposition to our faith that costs lives (Hebrews 12:4). Nevertheless, we live in a culture that opposes our faith more strongly and more openly every day. Help the participants discuss situations we might face at school or at work (or anywhere else) where our faith, like Susanna's, might be put to the test.

Remind participants to skim Ecclesiasticus for next time, looking for major themes. (They may find the outline and subheadings helpful for this assignment.)

2

Ecclesiasticus
(Wisdom of Jesus Son of Sirach)

Objectives

By the power of the Holy Spirit working through God's Word, participants will

- ◆ gain firsthand experience in answering why some books were included in the Bible and some were not;
- ◆ appreciate the positive role of women in the Bible; and
- ◆ learn to base their worldview (wisdom) on a solid, personal knowledge of the Lord and His Word (the fear of the Lord).

Why didn't God's people include Ecclesiasticus in the list of books that were recognized as holy? On the surface, the author seems well grounded in the Torah (the Hebrew Scriptures) and its application to daily life. However, a closer reading reveals several major flaws. First, Ecclesiasticus reflects a very negative view of women. The role of godly women in Proverbs and the major female figures of the Old Testament (such as Ruth, Deborah, and Esther) require a much more positive evaluation of women than we find in Ecclesiasticus. Second, the author seems to regard good works (such as almsgiving) as sufficient to atone for sins. The Old Testament clearly teaches that only death (blood sacrifice) atones for sins. Finally, some of the topics addressed seem a bit superficial (for example, table manners at banquets). We might agree that good manners are important, but that's not what convicts us of our sin or leads us to our Savior.

The Fear of the Lord

As session leader, you will want to help participants understand that the fear of the Lord includes both Law and Gospel. We can see how "fear" reflects saving faith from passages such as Acts 10:35. In that passage, "fears Him" denotes trust (justification) and "does what is right" refers to faithful obedience (sanctification). Together, they paint a complete picture of the child of God who trusts the Lord and acts accordingly.

15. Part of the idea communicated by the phrase "the fear of the LORD" is indeed an awareness of our accountability before God in judgment. This serves as a starting point for an appreciation of God's Word, particularly the third use of the Law (as a guide or template for Christian living). Our works do not save us from condemnation on Judgment Day, but they reflect the saving faith God has given us (see Matthew 25:31–46).

16. Hebrew poetry often rhymes the thought rather than the word-sound as does English. That is, a writer will paraphrase in the second line what he said in the first line. Mary offers us a good example of this approach in Luke 1:46–47, where verse 47 says essentially the same thing as verse 46 except for the added "my Savior" (she emphasizes this by adding it to the second line).

The phrase "knowledge of God" means more than merely knowing about God. It denotes a personal relationship with the Lord, such as Adam and Eve had before the fall into sin. Knowledge of God impacts every area of life, expressing itself in mercy and compassion toward others (see Hosea 6:6, quoted by Jesus in Matthew 9:13; 12:7).

17. In general, we may conclude that the author of Ecclesiasticus has a good grasp of the fear of the Lord. However, as session leader, you may want to invite the class members to talk about how it applies in the life of a believer. Jesus son of Sirach connects the fear of the Lord to the commandments of God (Ecclesiasticus 23:27) and seems to imply that the person who keeps these will always receive material blessing from the Lord (see Ecclesiasticus 2:10; 40:26). How, then, do we explain Job's great losses? We might conclude that Jesus son of Sirach's understanding of the fear of the Lord is somewhat mechanical and fails to take into

account God's will for the individual in the plan of salvation (see Joseph's analysis of his suffering and loss, Genesis 50:20; also 1 Peter 1:6–9).

18. By way of summarizing this part of the session on Ecclesiasticus, help participants flesh out their understanding of the fear of the Lord. Definitions should include trust, a real personal relationship with the Lord, submission to His will, and obedience to His commandments (motivated by a love and respect for Him). You may want to end with a case study from Scripture, illustrating what the fear of the Lord looks like. The story of the three young men in the fiery furnace (Daniel 3) or the story of Daniel and the lions' den (Daniel 6) would work well and would also lay a foundation for later sessions in the *Study Guide to the Apocrypha*.

Wisdom

The author of Ecclesiasticus, like the author of Proverbs, personifies wisdom. Rather than write about an abstract concept, the author creates a personal figure representing that concept. This technique helps the reader visualize the author's point and communicates more vividly. Ask the class participants in this session to consider how Ecclesiasticus differs from Proverbs and the rest of the Hebrew Scriptures in describing wisdom.

19. In both Ecclesiasticus and Proverbs, wisdom comes as a gift of God, the most desirable of all gifts. Help the participants conclude that wisdom is the understanding of how things work, both in heaven and on earth. The figure of wisdom knows how things really operate because she was the agent of God's creation. If you make something, you truly understand how it works.

It may be helpful to point out to class members that in many languages words have gender. A word may be masculine, feminine, or neuter, but these distinctions often have no connection to whether the thing represented by the word is male or female. When feminine pronouns are used of wisdom ("she," "her"), it doesn't mean that a female person is intended, only that the abstract noun is feminine. We will see in the next part that the author of Ecclesiasticus has a very low opinion of women, a view unrelated to the feminine gender of the noun *wisdom*.

20. The fear of the Lord is the beginning of wisdom because a real understanding of the world and how it works begins with an acknowledgement of the Lord as Creator and Ruler of the universe. Since He created everything and everyone, it makes sense that successful living begins with a familiarity with and respect for the One that put it all together.

21. As the three passages reveal, Jesus son of Sirach identifies wisdom as the Law of Moses. As session leader, invite the class members to discuss the positives and negatives of that connection. Biblically, wisdom is far broader than the Mosaic code. As Paul will later point out, the ultimate wisdom of God is Jesus Christ (1 Corinthians 1:24). You might also note that such a narrow definition of wisdom as the Mosaic Law could easily lead to legalism (see part 4 of this session, "Salvation").

Women

The Bible and world cultures often disagree with one another. Given the influence of Satan in the world and the sinful, self-willed nature of human beings, it cannot be otherwise. Every reader of Scripture therefore faces the challenging task of setting aside the values and worldview of the reader's own culture. We must first hear the Word of God clearly before we can then consider it and act on it. The author of Ecclesiasticus seems to allow his own feelings and the opinion of some of the people of his day to influence his evaluation of women. Lead the class members in discussing both his unbalanced view of women as well as our own difficulties in hearing God's Word clearly on this topic.

22. Lust has led many men to ruin. Remind the participants that the Bible is full of stories about men who let their lust for a woman lead them into all kinds of sin (for example, David and Bathsheba, 2 Samuel 11). You might also comment on the Muslim practice of covering a woman from head to toe in a burka to reduce the opportunity for lust. Some Muslim traditions even prohibit a woman from speaking in a soft or alluring voice to a man who is not her husband. Muslim law and tradition reflects very similar sensitivities and a worldview toward women as those which we see in Ecclesiasticus.

23. The author of Ecclesiasticus seems to see women negatively, evaluating them primarily as a risk to men. The Word of God praises the devout wife for her faith and her skill in managing her household (see Proverbs 31:10–29), an attitude noticeably lacking in Ecclesiasticus. His text has only faint praise for the godly wife and seems to give even that reluctantly (see chapter 26). We see the measure of his negative attitude toward women when he writes about daughters (22:3; 42:9–14).

24. The New Testament views women as equal recipients of salvation with men (Galatians 3:26–29) while reaffirming the family structure on earth—the husband is head and the wife is helpmate (see 1 Corinthians 11:3; Ephesians 5:21–33; 1 Peter 3:1–8).

Salvation

Holy Scripture shows us the cost and consequence of sin: the violent death of the sinner (Ezekiel 18:4; see Romans 6:23). The Mosaic code requires a number of blood sacrifices for the sins of the people: burnt offerings (Leviticus 1), sin offerings (Leviticus4), and especially the Day of Atonement (Leviticus 16). As Christians, we realize these never effectively dealt with sin and yet they pointed the way to the blood sacrifice that would pay for the sins of the whole world: Christ crucified (see Hebrews 10:1–18). The author of Ecclesiasticus has a different approach to the problem of sin and salvation.

25. The author of Ecclesiasticus believes people have free will and can choose to keep God's commandments, thereby earning salvation. Paul argues that we cannot keep the Law and, if judged by the Law, receive only condemnation. Even Christians, in their struggle to keep the Law, do it only imperfectly and frequently fall into sin.

26. The author of Ecclesiasticus seems to advocate a doctrine of double predestination, in which God predestines some to hell and others to heaven. Not only does this contradict his own position in chapter 15, but it also deviates from Scripture's comforting teaching that our election by God is anchored solidly and firmly in the cross of Christ. Those who face condemnation on the Last Day have only themselves to blame. Those who are raised to new life through faith in Jesus Christ, crucified and risen from the dead, have only God to thank.

27. Ecclesiasticus appears to offer no hope for life after death, nor does it teach the resurrection (see 17:27–28; 38:16–23). Perhaps Jesus son of Sirach, like the Sadducees, denied the resurrection. (See Jesus' response to the Sadducees on this question in Matthew 22:23–32. The class may also benefit from reading 1 Corinthians 15, the "resurrection chapter.")

28. Jesus son of Sirach did not consistently teach the biblical view of salvation but emphasized humankind's power to pursue personal righteousness. In contrast, Jesus Christ taught that the Hebrew Scriptures pointed to Him and prophesied His death and resurrection for the atonement of sins and the salvation of souls. (See Matthew 26:52–56; Luke 24:44–47; St. Paul affirms this in 1 Corinthians 15:3–4, where "according to the Scriptures" equals "as predicted in the Hebrew Scriptures.")

A Hymn in Honor of Our Ancestors

In Ecclesiasticus 44:1–50:24, the author opens with a call to praise the Lord and ends with a benediction, blessing his readers with a prayer for gladness of heart, peace in their lives, and deliverance in their day (50:22–24). Beginning with Enoch, he catalogues those men who lived at critical times in the salvation history of God's people. You, as session leader, might note two things: first, no women are included in this list, reflecting the author's negative attitude toward them; second, he chooses his examples carefully to make his point (as did Stephen before the Sanhedrin, Acts 7). These men show us how to live as God's people and how the Lord then blesses us when we do.

29. A *covenant* is a legally binding promise. Some covenants were unconditional, such as the promise never to send another great flood (Genesis 9:11). Others were conditioned upon the continued faithful obedience of the people, such as the covenant to occupy the Promised Land (see Deuteronomy 29). People commonly sealed a covenant with blood (the violent death of a sacrifice, as in Genesis 15:9–10). God ultimately seals His covenant of salvation with us in the blood of Jesus Christ, His Son, which we receive in the Lord's Supper.

30. Aaron, Phinehas, Samuel, and Simon all occupied the office of high priest. The author considers them important because he values the role of the high priest in the life of God's people. He sees the temple as the place of God's blessing and the high priesthood as the office through which that blessing comes to the people. Point out to class members that Jesus is the ultimate temple of God (see John 2:19) and the great High Priest (see Hebrews 7).

31. As session leader, help the class members talk about what they gained from reading Ecclesiasticus. The author sums up his book in his final prayer and his last bit of advice. He gives praise and thanks to the Lord for all His help and offers his readers the recommendation to continue the pursuit of wisdom, which always has a good outcome in God's economy.

By way of summary, you might point out that the author of Ecclesiasticus started out relatively close to Scripture with his understanding of the fear of the Lord and of wisdom, although you can already see he has begun to stray from God's Word at this point. His treatment of women reveals an obvious departure from the Bible, a direction he continues to take with his teaching on atonement. In the end, he brings us back to more solid ground. He reminds us to trust the Lord, follow His precepts, and give thanks for His deliverance.

Remind participants to review the outline for the Wisdom of Solomon and read through the ESV headings in the book so that it becomes familiar for next time.

3

The Wisdom of Solomon

Objectives

By the power of the Holy Spirit working through God's Word, participants will

- ◆ see more clearly the value of our faith, especially in those areas where faith and culture clash;

- ◆ grow stronger in the ability to stand firm under persecution and resist the allure of wealth, power, fame, and so on; and

- ◆ appreciate more fully the gift of salvation by grace through faith in Christ Jesus as we see the righteousness of God displayed in the ten plagues of the exodus.

Christians in the first few centuries of the present era found a lot to like in the Wisdom of Solomon. This may be, at least in part, because some of the same thoughts in this book appear also in the Bible (for example, compare Wisdom 13:10–19 on the foolishness of idols with Isaiah 49:18–20; 44:9–20; Romans 1:18–23). As you work through the Wisdom of Solomon, ask class members to comment on any parallels to Scripture that they see.

As session leader, you may want to help participants consider the trials and temptations faced by Christians today, not only in other countries but also in our own. As you read through the Wisdom of Solomon together, spend a few minutes identifying the points of conflict between our own culture and our Christian faith.

Righteousness (1:1–6:11)

32. Ask the members of the class to read 1 Corinthians 15. Paul argues that since Jesus physically rose from the dead, we also shall rise on Judgment Day. He reminds us at the end of the chapter that we have victory in Jesus Christ, crucified and risen for us (vv. 54–57)—but he draws his argument to its conclusion in verse 58, an encouragement to continue to do the work of the Lord because it really does matter.

33. The world has to hate the righteous person. Invite the class to look at John 7, where Jesus explains to His brothers that the world has to hate Him because He convicts the world of sin. A righteous person, simply by living the faith, generates opposition (1 John 3:12–13).

34. An expert in the Law asks Jesus that very question (Luke 10:25). Jesus responded with the story of the Good Samaritan (Luke 10:26–37). If we try to justify ourselves, we must act like a neighbor to everyone we encounter—a complete impossibility. Only one thing is needful: Jesus Christ (the point of Luke 10:38–42). Help the class participants talk about the difference between the righteousness of justification (Christ's right standing with God credited to us by faith) and the righteousness of sanctification (the life that flows from faith). Our own righteousness cannot save us (Romans 3:19–20).

Point out to the class that the one key element missing in the Wisdom of Solomon is the figure of a redeemer.

Wisdom (6:12–11:1)

35. Solomon ended up worshiping false gods in temples he built for his foreign wives. Wisdom, unguided by God's Word, becomes foolishness.

36. Although Israel would not have a king for four centuries, God gave Moses four rules the king must follow (not counting the fact that the king must be Jewish).

- ◆ He must not acquire a large number of horses.

- ◆ He must not acquire a large number of wives.

- ◆ He must not amass a fortune in silver and gold.

- ◆ He must write out by his own hand a copy of Scripture to read and study all his life.

Solomon failed on all four counts. He had thousands and thousands of horses (1 Kings 4:26), tons and tons of gold (1 Kings 10:14), and a thousand wives and concubines (1 Kings 11:3). There is no record of Solomon writing out a copy of Scripture or studying it.

37. Wisdom provides the key to successful living because it denotes the understanding of how things really work, both in the spiritual as well as in the physical world. In the Bible, wisdom begins with trust in the Lord and submission to His will (Psalm 111:10). It flows from His Word, particularly His revealed will to Israel (Deuteronomy 4:5–6). Although Eve and Adam desired it (Genesis 3:6), it comes to human beings only as a gift (as for Solomon, 1 Kings 5:12; see also Psalm 51:6). It is characteristic of the Messiah (Isaiah 11:2; Luke 2:40), who is ultimately the wisdom of God incarnate (1 Corinthians 1:20–25).

God's Justice (11:2–19:22)

The author of the Wisdom of Solomon wants his readers to know that they will be better off with the Lord than with the religion of the surrounding culture. He asks them to consider the exodus and its ten plagues (Exodus 7–11).

38. The Nile flooded annually, leaving a rich deposit of silt, which, when farmed, produced excellent crops. It was the lifeblood of the region. Ironically, God turned it to blood in the first plague (Exodus 7:14–24). Two additional points: first, the life of an animal or of a person is in the blood (Genesis 9:4–5); second, the Egyptians had decreed the death of Hebrew male babies. Their attempt to turn life into death justified the Nile's transformation from life (water) to death (blood).

39. The Egyptians worshiped a variety of creatures in their polytheistic religion. The plagues involving these animals and insects sent them a surplus of the things they worshiped. By doing so, the Lord demonstrated His absolute power over all nature (see Paul's condemnation of idolatry, Romans 1:18–23).

40. God outlined His plan to Abraham in Genesis 15:12–16. In danger of assimilation in Canaan, the descendants of Abraham could multiply safely in Egypt since the Egyptians didn't much like foreigners and they detested shepherds (Genesis 43:32; 46:33–34). Paul points out

that God finally and fully punishes all sins at the cross (Romans 3:21–26).

41. Not only does worship of creation violate the First Commandment (Exodus 20:3–6), but it also has two additional problems: first, it is foolish to worship things lower in the order of creation than you are (God created humankind to rule creation); second, God holds us accountable. Readers of the Wisdom of Solomon should remember that nature worship didn't work out at all well for the Egyptians at the time of the exodus. The Lord is King of all creation.

42. The Lord wanted Israel to learn what it means to be a child of God. Direct class members to Deuteronomy 8, where Moses unpacks Exodus 16. The lesson? A child of God "does not live on bread alone, but . . . by every word that comes from the mouth of the LORD" (Deuteronomy 8:3). That is, we focus on God's Word and will, not on our own welfare. (See how Jesus uses this passage, Matthew 4:4.) Their hunger could have led them to stronger faith and faithful living. Their complaints and their attempts to hoard the manna revealed the failure of their faith.

43. The incident involving the bronze serpent highlights the danger of graven images. Even though the people knew that it was God, not the bronze serpent, who rescued them, they eventually worshiped it and make sacrifices to it. Over seven hundred years later, King Hezekiah had it broken into pieces (2 Kings 18:4). Jesus uses the figure of the bronze snake as a preview of His own crucifixion, being lifted up so that those who "looked up" might be saved through faith in Him (John 3:14–15).

44. Isaiah directs us to the Word of God (8:20; *testimony* is used as a synonym for the Law, particularly the Ten Commandments). He then identifies the light as the Messiah, whose coming breaks the darkness with light, life, and hope (Isaiah 9:6–7). Jesus begins His ministry in Galilee as a fulfillment of this prophecy (Matthew 4:14–16). Jesus identifies Himself as the light and life of the world (John 8:12; 9:5).

45. We also have a High Priest who intercedes for us and makes atonement for our sins (Hebrews 4:14–5:10). Jesus offered Himself as the price required by the Law for atonement (Hebrews 9:26–28).

46. The enemies of Jesus used the cross to silence Him and disperse His followers. Crucifixion reflects God's curse (Deuteronomy 21:22–23; see Galatians 3:13–14 for application of that passage to the cross). As session leader, you might have the class look at Wisdom 19:22 and then turn to Romans 8:28–39. The way of folly leads to death. The way of wisdom leads to life eternal.

Remind participants to skim over both Judith and Tobit for next time, taking time to read Judith 16 and Tobit 13.

4

Judith and Tobit

Objectives

By the power of the Holy Spirit working through God's Word, participants will

- become more sensitive to the efforts of these authors to encourage the people of their day to keep the faith;
- consider ways we can positively impact Christians in our own era to remain faithful; and
- grow in the ability to see why some books were recognized as Scripture and others were not, even though they were often helpful to God's people.

The two compositions in this unit differ significantly from each other, but they also share a common bond. Their authors want readers to stay strong in their faith no matter what opposition they face. The author of Judith offers us a fictional story about a heroine who acts decisively to save her village from idolatry and foreign invasion. Tobit presents a picture of a pious man who suffers for his faithfulness but, by angelic intervention and magic, comes out just fine.

Judith

47. Direct the students to the study notes in *The Apocrypha: The Lutheran Edition with Notes* as well as any other resources you may have available. The author of Judith paints a picture of the "baddest bad guy" imaginable, drawing on Old Testament history to some extent. If Judith succeeds against this ultimate enemy, then readers can prevail in their struggle for the faith—if they trust God and act on their faith.

48. Holofernes, the arch-villain of the story, comes to Israel under orders to destroy the people of the region. You might use the historical analogy of Sherman's "March to the Sea" (November 15–December 21, 1864) in the American Civil War to help participants visualize Holofernes's campaign.

49. The author reveals the point of contact between the story of Judith and his readers in 3:8. If people would deny their faith and worship Nebuchadnezzar, they would save their lives and their cities.

50. Joakim, the (fictional) high priest in Jerusalem, calls the people to prayer and repentance. They turn to the Lord for salvation, but they do not wait passively for His answer. Like King Leonidas at the Battle of Thermopylae (480 BC; the last stand of the three hundred Spartans), Joakim writes to the residents of Bethulia and another town to block the only pass to Jerusalem. Faith combined with action, as readers will see, results in rescue.

51. Achior points out to Holofernes (and to the readers of Judith) that God's people have always survived as long as they remained faithful to the Lord (5:17–18).

52. Holofernes lays siege to the town, shutting off its water supply (7:12–13). You might point out to the participants that the plan worked very well. The people gave up hope in God and prepared to give up their faith as well (see 7:25; contrast their response to the faith of the three Jewish men in Daniel 3:16–18). At this point, the author introduces the heroine: Judith.

53. Simeon (along with Levi), deceived and murdered the men of Shechem after their prince (also named Shechem) assaulted their sister. This was problematic because they had agreed to give their sister to Shechem as wife following the assault. It was, therefore, a breach of covenant.

54. Judith confirms Achior's story and then gives Holofernes a believable reason to think the Lord will abandon His people: in their hunger and thirst, they are about to eat the food reserved for priests (Judith 11:11–15; see Numbers 18:8–32).

55. Judith beheads Holofernes when he passes out from too much wine. Like Jael, she kills the sleeping enemy general (Judges 4:21). Like Samson, she prays for heroic strength to kill the enemy (Judges 16:28–30). Like Deborah, she leads her people (chapter 14; Judges 4:9). The severed head and the bed canopy prove her story when she returns.

Tobit

As session leader, consider asking the class to look at Deuteronomy 21:22–23. A criminal's body was publicly displayed by hanging it on a tree after execution, postponing burial. However, the Lord required burial of the body before sundown to avoid defiling the land with an unburied body. You might add that in Roman times, crucified bodies were ordinarily left to rot on the cross, adding to the shame and dishonor. When Nicodemus and Joseph of Arimathea asked permission to bury Jesus' body (John 19:38–39), they risked their own lives. Pilate, convinced of Jesus' innocence, let them bury Him.

56. Tobit triple-tithed (gave thirty percent) when he lived in Jerusalem and even kept the kosher food laws when in captivity. He tells us that he continued to give to the poor and even buried the dead Jews executed by the state, though it cost him everything he owned (he had to fled his home and he lost his property).

57. Tobit goes blind and ends up with his wife supporting him. Like Job's wife, Tobit's wife challenges his faith (2:14). As in every good story, the darkest hour comes just before the dawn.

58. Tobit and his wife prayed to the Lord, who dispatched the angel Raphael to help them. Readers would get the point: pray to God, especially when you are at your darkest hour, and He will deliver you.

59. The author of Tobit advocates the "negative golden rule," much like Rabbi Hillel (first century BC), who said, "That which is hateful to you, do not do to your neighbor" (Babylonian Talmud, tractate Shabbat 31a). Jesus proposes a much higher standard: do not merely avoid harming your neighbor, but do for him or her everything you would want done for you. (Luther's explanation of the Fifth Commandment includes both negative and positive ethics.)

60. The odor of burning fish heart and liver drives away the demon from Sarah's bedchamber (8:2–3). Liquid from the fish's gallbladder cures Tobit of his blindness (11:10–13). The story of Tobit is fictional, but even in the Bible the Lord uses misunderstandings of His people to accomplish His goals. Direct the class members to Jacob's use of tree branches to affect the coloring of lambs and goats in Genesis 30:37–43. Even Jacob recognizes God's hand at work in Genesis 31:9.

61. Scripture clearly teaches that we are saved by grace through faith in the Lord and His Messiah alone. The author of Tobit doesn't really engage the theme of grace in his book, creating a tension for Christian readers. However, as session leader, you can open a discussion of the value of good works, remembering that all good works flow from a living faith. Good works cannot save anyone (Romans 3:19–20), but they matter because God cares for His children (see Matthew 25:31–46).

62. Both Judith and Tobit include a prayer of praise and thanksgiving to God for all His wonderful deeds because it is the appropriate thing to do following deliverance. We do this privately, of course, but we also do it when we worship corporately.

This point provides the session leader with the opportunity to talk about worship and why we use a liturgy. In it, God reaches out to us with salvation (Word and Sacrament), and we respond with prayer, praise, and thanksgiving. You might note for the class participants that God established the Sabbath for this very reason: to rest our bodies (Exodus 20:8–11) and to rest our souls (Deuteronomy 5:12–15), recounting His acts of deliverance. For Old Testament believers, this was the exodus. For New Testament children of God, it is Christ crucified and risen for the forgiveness of our sins. When we come to public worship, we confess our faith to the whole world, receive the blessing of the Lord in Word and Sacrament, and offer prayer, praise, and thanksgiving to the God who has called us together in faith.

Remind participants to read the Letter of Jeremiah and Bel and the Dragon. They should also familiarize themselves with the biblical account of Esther for next time.

5

Baruch, the Letter of Jeremiah, Old Greek Esther, and Bel and the Dragon

Objectives

By the power of the Holy Spirit working through God's Word, participants will

- ◆ see the need for regular confession and absolution in the life of a child of God;

- ◆ understand that idolatry is alive and well in our culture today; and

- ◆ appreciate the role of sanctified reason (that is, reason guided by faith) in interacting with pagan culture.

Baruch

God's people have always faced the temptation to take God and their elect status for granted (see Paul's warning, 1 Corinthians 10:1–13). The Jerusalem temple, like the tabernacle before it, was a kind of embassy of heaven on earth. Similarly, even though foreign embassies are on American soil, the land connected to the embassy is legally foreign soil. If we cross the threshold of the German embassy in Washington DC, we legally enter the sovereign territory of Germany. God dwelt in His embassy, the temple, which housed the ark of the covenant and other artifacts. As a result, people made the mistake of thinking they could worship other gods and act contrary to God's Word and still avoid disaster because God *had* to protect His temple (Jeremiah 7:3–14). They were wrong.

They refused to repent, turn to the Lord, and seek forgiveness for their idolatry and immorality. Consequently, following God's warning centuries earlier to Moses (Deuteronomy 28), Jerusalem fell to the Babylonians, and they destroyed the temple in 587 BC.

What went wrong? Baruch draws on the Hebrew Scriptures to show his readers that God, faithful to His covenant, did not do them any injustice by raising up the Babylonians and giving Jerusalem into their hands. Rather, responsibility falls squarely on the people. If his readers will confess their sin, God will forgive them and restore them to a place of peace and blessing. Faithfulness to His Word is the key to survival and recovery.

63. Baruch calls God's people to confess their sin and admit their ownership of the disaster experienced by Jerusalem and the temple. As session leader, you might point out that we do the same thing at the beginning of our liturgy. For many centuries, Christians have begun their worship by admitting their sin and seeking forgiveness from God. Such confession lays the groundwork for forgiveness (absolution) and entrance into God's presence (represented by the Introit and the remainder of the liturgy). Ask class participants to read Daniel's prayer in Daniel 9:4–19.

64. Baruch offers a number of reasons for God's intervention: the Lord had rescued them before, so why not again? (Exodus 12); God was inclined toward mercy (Exodus 20:6); God had a reputation among the Gentiles to protect (Exodus 32:11–14); God's glory was tied to Jerusalem, its temple, and its residents. You may want to discuss the glory of God with class members. Be sure to mention that *glory* ordinarily refers to "reputation or opinion others have of you." The Bible often uses *glory* to refer to the radiant majesty of God, but it can also designate God's saving acts, especially the cross. The chief glory of God is the salvation of sinners.

65. Baruch directs his readers to God's Word in the search for wisdom. At the same time, he points out that the depth of wisdom and its mysteries lie far beyond our reach. Only God understands wisdom (see Job 28, esp. v. 23). However, the Lord has revealed His Word to us, and in Holy Scripture we find wisdom for living as His people. (You might direct the class members to Deuteronomy 6:1–8.) God wants His

people to connect to His Word so that it will be always in their thoughts, direct their deeds, and serve as the foundation for their homes.

66. God did not destroy them; He only disciplined them for their own good when He handed them over to the Babylonians (and other, later, oppressors). This theme often appears in both Old and New Testaments (see Deuteronomy 8:5; Hebrews 12:10). Their time of discipline will end, and the Lord will lead them back home in glory.

67. Readers can find blessing in Baruch in the following ways: realizing that Confession and Absolution are a necessary part of our lives; understanding that the Word of God continues to instruct us in faith and faithful living; and finding real comfort in the promise of salvation and restoration, ultimately given at the Last Day in the resurrection to eternal life through Jesus Christ.

The Letter of Jeremiah

The prophets Jeremiah (active from 628–587 BC) and Isaiah (about a century earlier than Jeremiah) had written extensively about the foolishness of idols and the deception inherent in them. The people had not listened but had persecuted the prophets for telling the truth. The author of this letter tries again to convince his readers that idols and the religions that use them lead only to death and destruction.

68. People turned to idols for help, but to no avail. Idols embodied lies because they could not help themselves, much less anyone else. As session leader, you might point out that Jeremiah wrote the biblical book that bears his name in Hebrew, except for one verse—Jeremiah 10:11. That verse is in Aramaic (the international language of diplomacy at that time in the Near East), because Jeremiah wanted all the nations to hear the ultimate failure of idols. Human beings created them from the materials of this world, and along with the world they will pass away. They can offer no eternal help whatsoever.

69. Ask class members to imagine that they have a throne in the center of their hearts. Who or what sits on that throne in their lives? In other words, what is most important to them? Money, power, fame, drugs, and so on—these can all take the highest place in our lives and will all let us down eventually. Like wooden and stone idols of the past, modern idols lie to people by promising fulfillment, purpose, and

happiness, but in the end, they pass away. Ask participants to read Jesus' remarks in Matthew 6:19–34. As children of God through faith in Jesus Christ, what should our priorities be?

Old Greek Esther

The session leader for this part might want to review the historical overview of *The Apocrypha: The Lutheran Edition with Notes* regarding the Persian Empire (pp. xlvii–li) and check the map of the area occasionally (p. liii). You may want to read the biblical Book of Esther before leading the session on Old Greek Esther. The fact that the author of biblical Esther never explicitly mentions God explains why Jewish rabbis sometimes had trouble deciding whether this book was part of Holy Scripture or not.

70. In the daily course of our lives, we usually don't see God at work in an obvious way. This may explain the lack of divine reference in the biblical Book of Esther. Ask the class members to consider whether the author of biblical Esther left out the name of God as a literary device to reflect the lives we ordinarily lead. We know God rules the world and works to save people, but He seems to work behind the scenes more often than not. Biblical Esther incorporates this fact of life into the narrative, showing the reader that the Lord saved His people from destruction through seeming coincidence and timing.

71. Biblical Esther describes Haman as an Agagite, most likely an Amalekite, long-standing enemies of the Jews from the Negeb (see Numbers 13:29; 1 Samuel 15). Old Greek Esther changes his nationality to Bougean/Macedonian. During the period of the Persian Empire, Macedonia posed no threat to Persians or to the Judeans. By the mid-second century BC, the Ptolemies and Seleucids (both of Macedonian descent) had ruled Judea, often very harshly, for several centuries. Changing Haman's nationality aligns the story of Esther so it conforms to the world of the second century BC. He is an enemy everyone can hate.

72. Mordecai's dream updates the story of Esther to the type of Jewish literature common in the second century BC through the first century AD. It ties together the events of the story of Esther and credits the rescue of the Jewish people to the Lord's intervention (contrast the

Persian king's response to Esther in chapter 15, esp. v. 8, with the account in the biblical Book of Esther, chapter 5).

73. Old Greek Esther tells its readers that God will intervene and save them if they stay faithful to Him, do what He commands, and reject the pressure and allure of the Gentiles (see especially Esther's prayer, chapter 14). Biblical Esther makes its point much more subtly. For God's people, things seem somehow to work out all right. Only with the eyes of faith can the reader see the hand of the Lord behind all the "coincidences"—just like in real life.

Bel and the Dragon

Like the original audience of this three-part addition to Daniel, Christians find themselves living in the midst of a pagan culture. We face similar pressure and temptation to be inclusive: to coexist with other faiths by adopting the teaching that all religions lead to the same god. As session leader, you may want to start with a discussion of "the scandal of particularity": the stumbling block that Christians claim the only way to salvation is Jesus Christ, crucified for our sins and risen for our salvation (John 14:1–6). You might point out that all religions, except Christianity, do lead to the same "god"—Satan.

74. Daniel knows that Bel is "clay inside and brass outside" (v. 7) and that inanimate objects do not eat. Faith and reason together lead Daniel to the conclusion that someone is sneaking into the temple and consuming the food when no one is watching. The ashes on the floor reveal the footprints of those who deceive in the name of the idol.

75. Both stories make the same point that idols are lifeless things, foolish and unworthy objects of worship. Both stories end in the death of the idol's priests, a sober reminder of idol worship's ultimate end. However, in 1 Kings 18, God intervenes directly to reveal His presence, whereas in Bel and the Dragon, Daniel demonstrates his point by sanctified reason. Christian apologists still use this approach in defending the faith.

76. Daniel combined pitch, fat, and hair to produce a lethal mixture for the dragon. *Pitch* denotes a combustible substance, perhaps petroleum based (see Prayer of Azariah 23). *Fat* refers to a variety of compounds, many of which are flammable. Whale blubber, for example,

was harvested for multiple purposes, including the production of candles and oil for lamps. Hair, likewise, is highly flammable. Although it might seem like a stretch of the imagination, Daniel's "science project" might have been an early incendiary device ignited by the chemicals in the snake's (or dragon's) digestive tract. Again, Daniel uses the gifts God has given him (a sharp intellect) to prove the foolishness of idols, even living ones.

77. In both accounts, the king throws Daniel into the lions' den because others pressure him to do so. In both stories, the lions refrain from eating Daniel even though they are hungry. In the biblical Book of Daniel, the king tosses Daniel into the den because Daniel refuses to pray in secret to the true God and publicly avoids praying to the king. Daniel survives the night in the biblical story, but in this addition, he survives six nights. You might mention that the other obvious difference (meal provided by Habakkuk) may have been added because Habakkuk was a very popular prophet during the second and first centuries BC. Of the three parts in the addition, this is the only time God directly intervenes. Daniel's enemies perish at the end of this addition as well as in biblical Daniel. The point of the story is that idols cannot help their adherents, but the Lord rescues people that trust Him and follow His commandments.

Remind participants to skim 1 Maccabees and review the book's outline, looking for main characters for next time.

6

1 Maccabees

Objectives

By the power of the Holy Spirit working through God's Word, participants will

- ◆ grow in understanding the mindset of the Jewish people in the New Testament by studying the forces that forged it;
- ◆ appreciate the sacrifice that faith in the Lord and faithfulness to His Word can entail; and
- ◆ become better prepared to face the world's opposition by faith.

Review the historical material covering the time of Alexander the Great through the period of the Maccabees (pp. lv–lxxv). To help class members from being overwhelmed with the strange places and people, concentrate on a few important figures. Highlight the impact of Alexander the Great, Antiochus IV Epiphanes, and the Maccabean family.

The Problem (Chapter 1)

78. Alexander's conquest of Israel (and the rest of the Mediterranean world) left a legacy of Greek culture and language. A form of "common Greek" (Koine, the Greek of the Septuagint and the New Testament) spread across the region, making it possible to communicate anywhere in the area no matter what language a person spoke back home. (See p. lvii of *The Apocrypha: The Lutheran Edition with Notes*, which lists four beneficial effects of Alexander's conquest.)

79. Antiochus IV Epiphanes wanted to unite his subjects by converting them to Greek culture, language, and religion (Hellenization). Thinking himself divine, he wanted people to worship him as the chief god of the Greek pantheon, Zeus (see p. lxvi of *The Apocrypha: The Lutheran Edition with Notes*; 1 Maccabees 1:43–49).

80. Antiochus IV banned circumcision (a sign of God's covenant) and the Torah. As session leader, you might point out that many Jewish males sought to undo their circumcision through medical means. Since athletic activities (always male only) were done nude, Jews were readily identifiable. The danger was that if circumcision and the Torah could be eliminated, the Jewish people would be assimilated into the Greek culture and cease to exist as God's people.

81. This "desolating sacrilege" (often translated as "the abomination of desolation") is an offering of an unclean animal to a false god on the altar of the holy temple in Jerusalem. Daniel foretold it (Daniel 11:31) and Jesus refers to it in Matthew 24:15. Given the etymology of the Greek word for *abomination* or *sacrilege*, you might explain to class participants that it refers to "a terrible smell that clears the room of people." Contrast this picture with those sacrifices that are acceptable to God, offered in faith. The Bible describes them as a "pleasing aroma" to God (see Genesis 8:21; Exodus 29:18).

Mattathias Reacts (Chapter 2)

82. Ask the class participants to look at the study notes for a start. Moses records the story of Phinehas and Zimri in Numbers 25 as an example of zeal for the Lord and His honor. Because Phinehas acted so decisively, the Lord did not put an end to their priestly line (Numbers 25:11). The author wants readers to know that Mattathias and his family are true descendants of Phinehas (grandson of the first high priest, Aaron) in lineage as well as in spirit. Mattathias shows us what "faith on fire" looks like.

83. The author of Maccabees omits any reference to the resurrection to eternal life that is the hope of every child of God, in both the Old and New Testaments. He mentions that Elijah was taken up into heaven (v. 58), but doesn't elaborate. The best Mattathias can offer is "great

honor and an everlasting name" (2:51). It may be that the author of
1 Maccabees, like the later Sadducees, rejected the physical resurrection.

84. God forgives; human beings get even. We respond to real or
imagined wrongs with violence, paying back for every injury or insult
received. Mattathias speaks honestly, reflecting the suffering of his
people at the hands of the Gentiles who persecuted them so fiercely.
Jesus challenges us to forgive others as we have been forgiven and warns
us of the consequences if we do not (see the Lord's Prayer, Matthew 6:9–
15). Lead the class in talking about the challenge of Christian
discipleship and the help offered by prayer, God's Word, and the
fellowship of other Christians.

Judas Maccabeus (3:1–9:22)

85. The Jewish festival of Hanukkah celebrates the dedication of the
temple by Judas Maccabeus in 164 BC after it was desecrated by the
Gentiles three years earlier. Also known as the "Festival of Lights,"
Hanukkah celebrations last for eight nights. Although 1 Maccabees does
not mention it, Jewish tradition records that only one sealed jar of olive
oil was found after reclaiming the temple. Ordinarily enough for one
night, it provided sufficient oil for all eight nights (the "miracle of the
oil"). Since Hanukkah falls near Christmas, many of the class
participants may have heard of it. This part of 1 Maccabees provides the
historical background for the holiday.

86. The author of 1 Maccabees legitimizes the Maccabees as leaders
in Israel by God's design. He keeps the reader's eye focused on
Mattathias and his descendants rather than on the Lord, supporting the
claim that the Maccabees and their descendants are the only rightful
rulers and high priests in Judea.

87. Mattathias had promised that zeal for the Law would result in
"great honor and an everlasting name" (2:51; see also the account of
Eleazar, 1 Maccabees 6:44). Judas and his family achieved that goal and
secured rights to the priesthood by their faithfulness to the Jewish laws.
Paul likewise had great zeal for the Law, leading him to persecute the
Church. Later, he understood that this persecution of Christ's followers
made him the foremost of sinners (1 Timothy 1:12–15).

88. Judas fears people will think him a coward if he withdraws from battle (9:10). In hindsight, we might suggest that the welfare of his followers should have outweighed concern for his reputation (9:23–27).

Jonathan (9:23–12:53)

89. The sons of Jambri, apparently a nomadic tribe that occupied territory along the route Jonathan traveled, ambushed him and killed him (9:35–36). Jonathan is the third of Mattathias's sons to fall in battle (as did Eleazar, 1 Maccabees 6:43–44). As session leader, you may want to continue the discussion of using violence to combat violence and the wisdom of "getting even."

90. After failing several times to defeat Jonathan in battle, the Syrian-Greek general Bacchides agreed to a peace treaty with Jonathan and left the country (9:58–73). He showed something of his brutality when he executed a number of Hellenistic Jewish supporters out of frustration and anger over Jonathan (9:69).

91. Jonathan becomes high priest by the appointment of Alexander Balas, who ruled the region from 154–145 BC (10:18–20). Shamefully, the office of high priest became a political prize that could be awarded by Gentiles. The Lord had appointed the first high priest, Aaron (Exodus 28:1–2), and high priests were supposed to serve for life. Only legitimate descendants of Aaron could be high priests.

92. Jonathan fought his share of battles, showing something of the military talent and skill of his brother Judas Maccabeus. His real gift, however, was reading the winds of political change. In an era where new claimants to the throne appeared almost daily, you needed to pick the winning side as an ally if you wanted to live. Even so, he eventually trusted the wrong man and fell victim to betrayal (12:46–48).

93. The Maccabees use military might and political savvy to suppress Gentile influences in their nation. When references to the Lord or to Holy Scriptures do appear, they seem to be more in the background. The references in 1 Maccabees 12:9, 15, for example, occur in a letter to Sparta. You might point out to class members that religious leaders would later charge Jesus with violating Jewish laws (Mark 2:24) and speaking against the temple (Matthew 26:61). These are the same charges Stephen faced at his trial (Acts 6:13).

Simon (Chapters 13–16)

94. Simon finally conquered the Akra (a citadel within the walls of Jerusalem, occupied by a pro-Greek faction). He also defeated a number of fortified cities that could have served as staging areas for future military action against the Jews. Faithful to Jewish laws and supportive of the temple (14:14–15), he brought the people together, healing some of the earlier divisions. Internationally, Simon reaffirmed bonds with Sparta and Rome, winning recognition of his dynasty from the Roman Republic around 139 BC.

95. The people proclaimed Simon their high priest forever (establishing his dynasty in that office, 1 Maccabees 14:41–49) and confirmed him as their military and political leader.

96. Simon's son-in-law, Ptolemy (son of Abubus), murdered him and two of his three sons at the end of a banquet held in their honor (16:14–16).

97. The Samaritans expected a messiah like Moses, a teacher who would restore things to the way they were. Jesus could reveal Himself to them without running the risk of starting a war. The violent history of the Jewish people in the first and second century BC and the idealized role of the Maccabean family helped shape messianic expectations in Judea. During the public ministry of Jesus, many expected a messiah like Simon—a warrior king and high priest who upheld the Jewish laws, supported the temple, and ended foreign domination.

Remind participants to skim over 2 Maccabees and then read the Prayer of Azariah, the Song of the Three Holy Children, and the Prayer of Manasseh for next time.

7

2 Maccabees and the Prayers and Songs

Objectives

By the power of the Holy Spirit working through God's Word, participants will

- understand that we try to conform our lives to God's Word because we are baptized into Christ Jesus and born into a new way of life (Romans 6:1–14);

- see in the person of Jesus Christ the ultimate dwelling of God, completely replacing the temple in Jerusalem as the place God and man come together; and

- accept that suffering for our faith, even to the point of death, serves God's plans for us and for the Church (1 Peter 1:3–9).

The author of 2 Maccabees believes that God's people can secure material blessings and victory over enemies by keeping His commands and decrees. Help guide class participants in discussing how this works out today. Take time to read Psalm 73, perhaps as part of an opening devotion. There, the psalmist points out that only in the final judgment of God do we see the real blessing of patterning our lives after God's Word (compare Psalm 73:17 with Matthew 25:31–46).

2 Maccabees

98. The author of 2 Maccabees wants the Jewish colony in Egypt to return to the true faith, based on Jewish law and anchored in the Jerusalem temple. Only in that temple does the name of God dwell (see Deuteronomy 12:10–11; 16:2; 1 Kings 5:3–5). For that reason, the author wants the Jews in Egypt to celebrate Hanukkah (the Festival of Lights) and the Feast of Booths.

99. Simon (not a Maccabean), a captain of the guards in the Jerusalem temple, informed a nearby governor that the temple housed vast riches ripe for plunder. As session leader, you might point out that people sometimes stored their money in temples as a type of early bank (as in Delphi, Greece). Since kings always needed money for war, building projects, gifts, and so on, Seleucus IV sent Heliodorus to collect money from the temple. Because the people were faithful and the high priest at the time, Onias III, was righteous, God intervened and stopped the "bank robbery." He even converted Heliodorus in the process.

100. Antiochus IV Epiphanes invaded Jerusalem and robbed the temple (5:15–16). God permitted it because the high priest, Menelaus, sinned and because many of the people had abandoned the Jewish way of life for the Greek way. Their sins led God to allow the desecration of the holy temple, at least for a little while (5:17–18; see 4:14–17). In 2 Maccabees 5:19–20, the author spells out the principle involved: as the temple goes, so goes the nation.

101. Discipline, not punishment, was God's purpose in allowing the suffering of the Jewish people under Antiochus IV Epiphanes. Two features distinguish discipline from punishment: it lasts for a shorter period of time, and its purpose is reconciliation, not payment for transgression. As session leader, you may want to point out that Paul also distinguished discipline from punishment when he addressed problems with the celebration of the Lord's Supper in 1 Corinthians 11:27–32.

102. The Lord forbids consumption of pork in the Hebrew Scriptures, declaring it unclean (Leviticus 11:7). Faithful to the covenant, Eleazar chose death rather than eat pork. The mother and her seven sons in 2 Maccabees 7 made the same decision with the same result. Muslims do not eat pork for the same reason. Christians are free to eat pork (and other unclean foods) because Christ fulfilled the Law and declared all foods clean (also, see Acts 10:9–16).

103. Eleazar refused to fake compliance because it would have set a bad example for others. What kind of witness do we make? For example, when we go to a restaurant after worship services, how do we behave and how do we treat the employees? How we act and what we tip are a

witness to them about our faith. Like Eleazar, we want to consider the impact of our actions on others.

104. Judas Maccabeus used good tactics and strategy in his battle with Nicanor, but his secret weapons were the Holy Scriptures ("the holy book," 8:23) and trust in the Lord.

105. The painful and humiliating end of Antiochus IV Epiphanes is recorded in 2 Maccabees 9. The author makes a point of noting the justice inherent in the manner of Antiochus's death. As Paul writes in Galatians 6:7, "God is not mocked, for whatever one sows, that will he also reap."

106. The men who died in battle had "good-luck charms," figurines of idols, under their cloaks. A clear violation of the First Commandment (Exodus 20:4), their breach of the covenant resulted in their deaths. Draw the attention of the class to the intercessory prayers for the dead (12:42–45) and the study notes in *The Apocrypha: The Lutheran Edition with Notes*.

107. With a new Seleucid king on the throne, a Hellenistic priest named Alcimus makes his move to become high priest in Jerusalem. He convinces the new king that Judas Maccabeus is the problem and that killing him is the only solution. General Nicanor threatens to level the temple if the people do not hand over Judas Maccabeus for execution (14:33). The threat is neutralized when Judas defeats Nicanor in battle. The author connects Judas's victory to a vision he received prior to battle. The late high priest Onias III, interceding for the Jewish people even after his death, introduces Judas to the late prophet Jeremiah. Jeremiah awards Judas a sacred golden sword that Judas then uses to help win the battle. If you have extra time, ask the class members to read the study notes for 2 Maccabees 15 and evaluate the idea that the dead intercede for the living.

The Prayer of Azariah and the Song of the Three Holy Children

108. When we bless the name of the Lord, we give thanks and praise to God for the wonderful things He has done for us. Praise, adoration, thanksgiving, and acknowledgement of God as the giver of all good things come together in blessing the Lord. In the Bible, the phrase

"bless the LORD" or "bless the name of the LORD" often occurs in the context of salvation (see Psalm 113; 124; Luke 1:67–79).

109. When Israel turned its back on God, worshiped false gods, and promoted immorality, refusing to repent, God responded with the Law (Deuteronomy 28:15–68). He showed His mercy to His people at the time of the Babylonian captivity by not utterly destroying them and by promising to return a remnant of the people to the Promised Land after seventy years in Babylon (Jeremiah 25:11–12; 29:10). From this tiny group of returnees, the Lord would bring forth a deliverer for all people—Jesus Christ, Son of David and Son of God (Gospel).

110. When we find ourselves trapped in sin, the only way out is to confess our sin to the Lord and return to Him with a broken spirit and a contrite heart (Psalm 51:17). You might invite the class to read Psalm 51, written by King David after his affair with Bathsheba and the multiple murders he committed trying to cover it up (2 Samuel 11). Point out the frequent use of this psalm in our liturgies.

111. Like the three Jewish men (Daniel 3), Stephen made a powerful witness to his faith in a life-or-death situation. Unlike the three men in the fiery furnace, Stephen died at the hands of his accusers. Sometimes God rescues us from earthly peril (like the three Jewish men; see also Peter in Acts 12), and sometimes it serves the cause of the Gospel for us to die (like Stephen and James, brother of John, in Acts 12). For the child of God, it's a win-win situation. If we die, we get to be with the Lord. If we live, we live to serve Him here another day (see 2 Corinthians 5:1–10; Philippians 1:21–23).

The Prayer of Manasseh

112. Read 2 Kings 21:1–18 for a catalogue of Manasseh's crimes, including the sacrifice of his son in the fire to a false god (v. 6). While the patriarchs did sin, they did not sin against God in the arrogant, idolatrous, and violent way that Manasseh did. As he confesses his sin, we can certainly understand why he said what he did in verse 8 of his prayer. (For a New Testament parallel, read Paul's self-evaluation in 1 Timothy 1:12–17.) Allow time for the group to discuss any examples they would like to share.

113. God does not delight in the death of sinners. He wants them to repent, turn to Him, and live (see Ezekiel 18:23). You may want to have the class read Luke 15 and talk about the joy in heaven over one sinner who repents. God is as much a God of the "righteous" as He is of those who repent.

114. The author of the Prayer of Manasseh hits the nail on the head when he portrays Manasseh "bending the knees of his heart" (see v. 11). Ask class participants to read Jesus' story of the Pharisee and the tax collector (Luke 18:9–14). Help class members see the vital role that Confession and Absolution play in our personal relationship with God and our corporate worship together.